D1416931

We both know gifts don't mean much

compared to our love

and God's blessed touch . . . .

So the prayer for you to our Father above

is to keep you safe in His infinite love.

THE
Just Because
SERIES

Moments of Celebration

HELEN STEINER RICE

Fleming H. Revell
A Division of Baker Book House Co
Grand Rapids, Michigan 49516

© 2002 by Virginia Ruehlmann
and The Helen Steiner Rice Foundation

Published by Fleming H. Revell
a division of Baker Book House Company
P.O. Box 6287, Grand Rapids, MI 49516-6287

Poems taken from these books by Helen Steiner Rice, compiled by Virginia J. Ruehlmann: *Celebrating the Golden Years* (1998), *Daily Reflections* (1990), *A Book of Comfort* (1994), *A Book of Prayers* (1995), *God Bless America* (1991), *Christmas Blessings* (1991), *An Old-Time Christmas* (1997), *Our Family Treasury* (with Virginia J. Ruehlmann, 1998), *Gifts of Love* (1992), and *A Book of Thanks* (1993). Biographical information drawn from *Helen Steiner Rice: Ambassador of Sunshine* by Ronald Pollitt and Virginia Wiltse, published in 1994.

Printed in the United States of America

Library of Congress Cataloging-in-Publication Data is on file at the Library of Congress, Washington, D.C.

ISBN 0-8007-1799-6

Cover and interior design by Robin Black

For current information about all releases from Baker Book House, visit our web site:
http://www.bakerbooks.com

Celebrations, Moment by Moment

The Fourth of July without fireworks? Mother's Day without a rose? What would a holiday at hand be without these expected symbols?

Helen Steiner Rice was always looking for new icons and ways of celebrating what's on our calendars and in our hearts throughout her forty-two years as a poet and greeting card editor. Few holidays escaped her attention, or her pen, both on the job and on her own for an ever-increasing circle of friends.

From Martin Luther King Day and Valentine's Day, to Christmas and Easter, Helen found a thousand reasons for commemorating the holidays. Surprisingly, though, all the reasons were bound into a beautiful quilt by a thread of three cords: faith, hope, and love. With these ingredients every day can be a holiday, Helen believed, but all the more those enduring days marked on the calendar that we corporately anticipate and affectionately honor.

May you feel the quiet beauty
   of that holy, silent night
When God sent the little Christ Child
   to be this dark world's light.
May you know the peace He promised,
   may you feel His presence near,
Not only just at Christmas,
   but throughout a happy year.

— New Year's Day

As we start a new year
      untouched and unmarred,
Unblemished and flawless,
      unscratched and unscarred,
May we try to do it better
      and accomplish much more
And be kinder and wiser
      than in the year gone before.

New Year's Day

Taking this special time to say
you're thought about on New Year's Day
And wished a year that's richly blessed
with anything that's happiest,
And may God keep you in His care
and hear your every smallest prayer.

— New Year's Day